THIS BOOK BELONGS TO ...

100%
UNOFFICIAL

First published in Great Britain 2022 by 100% Unofficial,
a part of Farshore

An imprint of HarperCollins*Publishers*
1 London Bridge Street, London SE1 9GF
www.farshore.co.uk

HarperCollins*Publishers*
1st Floor, Watermarque Building, Ringsend Road
Dublin 4, Ireland

Written by Daniel Lipscombe
Illustrations by Matt Burgess

This book is an original creation by Farshore
© 2022 Farshore

ISBN 978 0 0085 0770 1
Printed in Spain
3

ONLINE SAFETY FOR YOUNGER FANS

Spending time online is great fun! Here are a few simple rules to help younger fans stay safe and keep the internet a great place to spend time.

- Never give out your real name – don't use it as your username.
- Never give out any of your personal details.
- Never tell anybody which school you go to or how old you are.
- Never tell anybody your password, except a parent or guardian.
- Be aware that you must be 13 or over to create an account on many sites. Always check the site policy and ask a parent or guardian for permission before registering.
- Always tell a parent or guardian if something is worrying you.

Stay safe online. Any website addresses listed in this book are correct at the time of going to print. However, Farshore is not responsible for content hosted by third parties. Please be aware that online content can be subject to change and websites can contain content that is unsuitable for children. We advise that all children are supervised when using the internet.

ROBLOX
ANNUAL 2023

CONTENTS

WELCOME TO THE ROBLOX ANNUAL 2023!

Roblox has had a fantastic year since the last time we were here. The platform keeps growing, gaining more players and, better yet, more games!

This is a celebration of the games that make Roblox one of the best platforms in the world. However, Roblox isn't only about playing the latest and greatest game; it's about friends and creativity too. So many of the great games we'll explore in this annual are designed for players like you to get together, which makes Roblox a great place to gather with your best gaming buddies.

It doesn't matter if you want to race the nicest cars, collect huge numbers of cute animals, or solve mysteries; your friends can always hop in and enjoy the experience too. It doesn't matter what kind of gamer you are; we'll make sure you find something you'll love to play.

We've got games for the sharpshooters among you, as well as games for those who prefer a quiet and relaxing experience, plus everything in between! Just flicking through the pages of this book, you'll see some games you've already played, some that are hugely successful and some hidden gems that we think you'll love.

So grab your friends, your controllers, keyboards and devices ...

IT'S TIME TO PLAY!

THE YEAR IN ROBLOX

The world of Roblox grows bigger every year and it became especially important as the world recovered from a pandemic. As everyone retreated indoors, Roblox helped keep people connected and even helped a few teachers hold classes for their pupils. Let's look at some of the exciting news from the past year on the platform.

HOME SCHOOLING

▓ As schools went in and out of lockdown, teachers, parents and pupils increasingly turned to Roblox to augment their educational needs. The Roblox Education section of the site saw a massive influx of learners working through the coding curriculum. There are even modules on staying safe online and learning how to be a good, civil Robloxian.

BUILD BETTER

▓ Roblox continued its regular series of Build It, Play It programs with the Mansion of Wonder, a magical interactive adventure that teaches users how to make particles in Roblox Studio. There are two different experiences, one for beginners and one for those who already know their way around the Studio, so everyone can join in the fun.

CREATIVE FORTUNE

▓ At the end of 2021, Roblox launched their Game Fund, which provided money to creators looking to make new games on the platform, particularly those that incorporated 'metaverse' items. It'll be a while before we see the awesome games that come from these schemes, but there are already some demos for funded games, such as Rolling Thunder.

LAYER UP

■ Avatars have been evolving year-on-year, especially since the Rthro character model was released. The latest innovation is layered clothing, which is currently still in beta on Roblox Studio. Basically this means you'll no longer have to choose between an awesome tee or a comfy hoody – you'll be able to layer your avatar with each one. Keep your eyes peeled for the full release soon.

EVENTS AND EXPERIENCES

▨ Away from the playing, lots of people gather in the game hubs to chat, dance and show off their avatars. Roblox has recently given us many more reasons to get together and emote. We've had rock concerts, rappers taking over in-game arenas and leading fashion designers showcasing wares on the platform. Even toys and movies got in on the Roblox action, building unique experiences to mess around within. There were even items and avatar clothing to collect if you joined in with the events!

THE 8TH ANNUAL BLOXY AWARDS

On Saturday March 27th, the annual Bloxy awards were held to celebrate the games, creators and communities from across the platform. Voting took place in the Bloxy hub and over 2.5 million votes were cast. Did some of your favourites win a Bloxy?

BEST NEW GAME

Brookhaven

MOBILE GAME OF THE YEAR

Super Golf!

BEST SLEEPER HIT

Super Doomspire

XBOX GAME OF THE YEAR

Phantom Forces

MOST EDUCATIONAL GAME

Lua Learning

MOST VISITS

Adopt Me!

GAME OF THE YEAR

Piggy

BEST OF THE BLOXYS

The Bloxy Awards started in 2013 as The Hall of Fame and focussed more on videos and trailers. In 2017, the awards were expanded to include games and the categories we recognise today. But is a Bloxy Award the peak for a game or is it just the beginning? Let's look at some previous winners of the Best Game award to see how they hold up today.

MURDER MYSTERY 2 — 2017

Still successful and highly played several years later, Murder Mystery 2 has twelve players enter the game – one sheriff, one murderer and ten innocent bystanders – and it becomes a hunt for the killer or a quest to stay alive, depending on which character you're given. Players loved this idea of being dropped into a murder mystery, so much so that in 2017 the game broke 500 million visits!

2018 — JAILBREAK

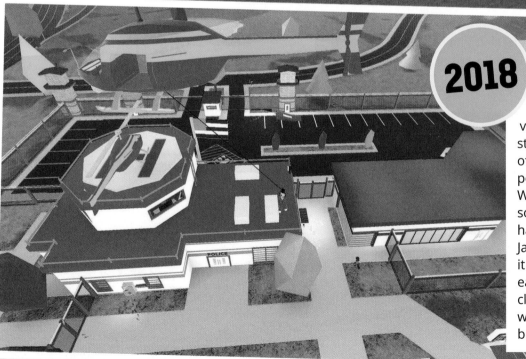

Thanks to its hugely versatile 'cops and robbers' style of play, Jailbreak is often considered the most popular game on Roblox. Why? Because even though some games nowadays have millions of players, Jailbreak has done that since it launched in 2017! And it's easy to see why – it's the classic combo of good vs bad, with fast cars and scrappy brawls thrown in.

BEE SWARM SIMULATOR

2019

Bee Swarm Simulator is the odd one out of this list – there are no fast cars, weapons or dangerous people hunting down players. It's just you and your bees, collecting pollen, talking to bears who hand out quests and lots of yummy honey. Millions of players jumped at the chance to bee-come beekeepers as it was so different and Roblox was buzzing about this sweet game.

2020 ## ARSENAL

There is no denying the popularity of first-person shooters in videogames. Many of the biggest games each year would slot into this category. So it's no surprise that Roblox picked Arsenal as the winner of the 7th Annual Bloxy award for Best Game. Arsenal does things differently, giving players random weapons after each point scored and urging you to try out all kinds of tactics to become the best player.

100

PIGGY

2021

The most recent winner of Best Game is one you'll have seen in the Top Games for months. PIGGY is a survival horror game where players must escape a location, avoiding the terrifying PIGGY. It became successful because it was a fun, scary game, but PIGGY has kept its millions of players by constantly expanding the story, adding new characters and rotating game modes to keep the game feeling fresh. Horror games are very popular on Roblox because who doesn't like being safely scared?

WHAT MAKES A GREAT
ROLE-PLAYING GAME?

Sometimes it can be hard to put your finger on exactly why you keep playing a game, so we're going to dive deep into some popular genres to find out what makes them tick and keeps players coming back for more. First up, it's role-playing games!

SOCIAL

■ An amazing feature of Roblox role-playing games is the social side. Most of them use the chat feature to allow players to trade items, set up mini-games, visit each other's houses or just explore the world together. It's a great way to stay connected with your mates, or even make new friends along the way.

HOUSES

■ Building and decorating houses is a huge part of the role-playing games on Roblox. It's a space where you can do whatever you want. With furniture to place, and paint and wallpaper to put on the walls, you can create your dream home! Showing off your home can be really fun, and buying new accessories lets you express yourself too.

DRESSING UP

■ Much like decorating your house, dressing up your avatar comes in handy when assuming a role. You can dress as you do offline, or become someone completely different. The idea of the game is to try out a new lifestyle that you never have before, whether that's where you live, who you hang out with, or what you do ...

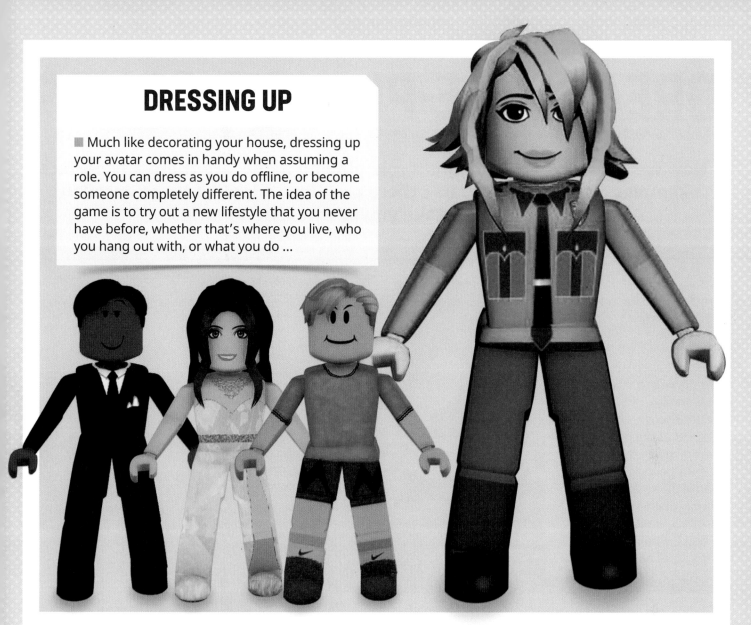

JOBS

■ If you want to buy all the fun items in these games, you will need money; and the best way to earn money is to enrol in a job. Some games offer jobs you would find offline: hairdresser, shop worker; while others can be much more fantastical: hero, villain or astronaut.

GREAT ROLE-PLAYING GAMES

Now we know the DNA of a great role-playing game, are there any perfect examples on Roblox? Of course there are! Have a look at these excellent games that can take you to whole new worlds.

BROOKHAVEN

▓ Brookhaven requires the players to take on a role and live it fully; you might choose to be a teacher at the local high school; perhaps you'd like to be a police officer and patrol the streets; or you may prefer to work in the hospital, treating other visitors, who will be playing the role of patients.

▓ When you arrive in Brookhaven, it's worth heading straight to the housing area and choosing where you'd like to build your home. Then you can set out to explore the town, decorate your home and choose a nice car to cruise around in. While you're exploring, keep an eye out for items that seem out of place, as they may lead to secret, hidden areas.

▓ You won't have to earn money in Brookhaven – most in-game items are free and available as soon as you join the game. So there's nothing holding you back from creating your dream life in Brookhaven – how will you choose to live it?

MEEPCITY

MeepCity is a place unlike anything else. A place where funny, furry creatures called Meeps live among people. They can be pets or companions, living alongside your avatar while you work or play in the city. Meeps feature in most of the mini-games, meaning that your Meep will race, run and fish alongside you. They can also be personalised in loads of different ways to make yours unique.

ROYALE HIGH

Role-playing games don't always have to be set within a city. Royale High drops you into a large high school, full of other players playing as teachers and students. The best bit? Everyone is a fairy! There are lessons to attend and games to play when the school day ends. Other areas open up at certain times, where you can role-play further with your friends – a beach house, a getaway island, a trading centre to swap items and even a Battle Royale arena.

BLOXBURG

Bloxburg is the place to be if you want to play mini-games. Each of the twelve jobs, once taken on, turn into fun games allowing you to earn money while you play. It has some unique features among its peers – your avatar's health and happiness is important and their mood changes depending on the actions that you take. A busy citizen is often a happy one though!

INCLUSIVE GAMING

Over the past year, Roblox has continued to involve members of the community, highlighting important topics and issues. When the world is a chaotic place, many people find a little piece of home in Roblox.

BLM

■ Racism has no place in the world and Roblox has been using their platform to educate and support. The official blog showcased black creators, who spoke about their games and their experiences within the community. Roblox is primarily about playing games together, but it's also a huge social space where people from all walks of life can come together. It's important to support each other and use these spaces to discuss difficult topics in order to learn and stand up to hate.

PRIDE

■ Pride month is a very important time for members of the LGBTQ+ community. Each year, Roblox hopes to create a safe space for people to be themselves, encouraging players to learn more about Pride and include their pronouns in their profile. It's time to be welcoming and accepting of others. Creators, players and Roblox employees take time to talk and play together and celebrate Pride.

ANTI-BULLYING

In late 2020 Roblox, took a stronger stand against bullying. Players were told, via the Roblox blog, ways they can help stamp out bullying and keep Roblox a safe place to play. With so many people playing the thousands of games, sometimes bullying can occur. So, what did Roblox advise?

● **Help a friend or others targeted by online hate.**

Either you or a friend can chat to the bully and tell them that you don't agree with how they are treating the person being bullied. Even a small act like this can help change the situation.

● **Always be cautious not to escalate any problems.**

Try to distract others and change the topic of conversation. If you're in a game, you can invite the bullied person to change game with you.

● **Resist the urge to retaliate.**

Stay strong and do not resort to using your own hurtful words. This could make the situation much worse or cause the bully to begin targeting you.

● **Make your world a better place.**

If you've experienced bullying, you know how it can make a person feel. Use your time online and offline to be kind to people and support them when they need it.

YOU CAN FIND MORE ABOUT STAYING SAFE ONLINE ON PAGE 68

WHAT MAKES A GREAT
MYSTERY GAME?

Mystery games come in all shapes and sizes. Whether it's solving a conundrum or hunting an imposter, they're usually created as multiplayer experiences, so they're perfect to play with friends. But the real mystery is what exactly makes a great mystery game?

TEAMWORK

■ With many mystery games, you will find yourself on a team of players. Be they friends or complete strangers, you will get the best experience by playing together. Whether you're solving a murder mystery or discussing who on your team might be betraying your efforts, use the in-game chat box to talk to others. This communication makes or breaks a game; without this chat, the game won't make sense. Also, working as part of a team will make for more memorable moments during the game. Working together to solve the problem feels great!

VARIETY

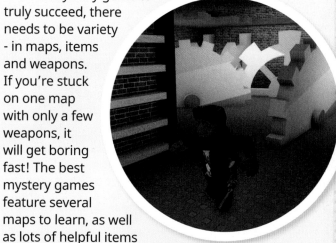

■ For a mystery game to truly succeed, there needs to be variety - in maps, items and weapons. If you're stuck on one map with only a few weapons, it will get boring fast! The best mystery games feature several maps to learn, as well as lots of helpful items that are used to solve the mystery. You'll find that most of the popular mystery games will also feature several roles to play as. You might be a witness to the murder, the killer themselves or a cop/sheriff who needs to hunt the murderer.

PUZZLES

■ Puzzles appear in several mystery games, sometimes as word quizzes or hidden item games. Completing these will usually reward you with a clue to help you solve the case, or maybe a helpful item that you can use to catch a killer. These puzzles can add a lot to a game and elevate it beyond just running and hiding around levels. Puzzles can also appear as mini-games, particularly in imposter game types.

BREAK IN

Break In is a multiplayer story game about being stuck in a house while chaos unfolds outside. You're locked in, and every day that passes will see some of the players eliminated. You'll be ranked on how well you survive and how you work with others, with all this building to a huge finale boss fight. While there isn't a mystery to solve, Break In requires a lot of working together, or double crossing each other if you fancy it. You will need to be sneaky and stick to your tasks, which can prove tricky when you know you might be eliminated next!

MURDER MYSTERY 2

In Murder Mystery 2, twelve players enter the game and are given a role. There is a killer, a sheriff and ten civilians. Winning the game can be achieved in different ways depending on the role you play. If you're the killer, you must eliminate all other players; as the sheriff, you need to catch the killer before time runs out; as a civilian, you'll need to hide, run and help the sheriff.

MURDER PARTY

Much like Murder Mystery 2, players of Murder Party find themselves assigned to a role within a group. But that's where the similarity ends. Murder Party features extra roles to play – such as the hacker, who must hide within the map and reveal the killer for everyone to see – and the games are played over smaller, wackier maps. Every round of this game feels like a party as so many people are dressed up and the maps feature lots of flashing lights and awesome animations.

HIDDEN GEMS

Every year in this annual, we like to look at and recommend some of the smaller games. These are the ones that don't always have thousands of players but are great fun. They're games that you might not spot on the front page of Roblox. Give some of them a try and see what you think.

DELIVERYMAN SIMULATOR

Inspired by strength-training games, Deliveryman Simulator asks players to deliver packages around a crazy land. Starting out, you'll need to carry the smallest boxes, gaining energy with each delivery. This energy can be used to build your avatar's strength and allow you to carry larger parcels. Bigger packages delivered faster equals more energy. At first the delivery routes are simple, but as the game goes on, each delivery gets tougher and longer. Working with a friend will reward players with more energy and some in-game items.

FARMING AND FRIENDS

Farming can be very relaxing – just driving across your farm, planting seeds and harvesting the crops. Farming and Friends starts you out with equipment and a crop of wheat to harvest and sell. With the money you make, you can buy different seeds for new crops, then take care of them using the machinery in your garage.

As you grow and sell more, you'll be able to buy bigger and better machines, and if you call in the help from friends, you can harvest faster and become the best farmer out there!

PILFERING PIRATES

In Pilfering Pirates, four teams of players start on a ship – green, red, blue or yellow. The aim of the game is to completely destroy the other ships. To do this, you can use cannons on your ship, or use the weapons in your inventory. Most weapons are explosive and deal lots of damage, so you can stay on your own ship and fire out rockets. Or you can build bridges to dash over to the enemy ship and sabotage it from inside. While you're there, you can pilfer any gold from the boat, which you can exchange for bigger and better weapons. The last surviving team wins the game and rules the seas!

STAY ON THE CUBE

Can you stay on a constantly spinning cube that slowly breaks into pieces over time? Stay on the Cube is almost a Battle Royale – all players start by standing on top of a giant cube. The cube could be solid, have a hollow middle or be filled with obstacles. Not long after starting the round, large bouncing balls begin to hit the cube, breaking away small chunks and spinning the cube faster, in several different directions. All you need to do is stay on or in the cube as long as you can. If you fall, you're out until the next round. It sounds simple, but it's a crafty game. Players can even use in-game money to launch more balls, larger balls or spin the cube in a new direction.

JUDY

JUDY is another in a long line of horror sensations. Starting on a fairground boat ride, which trundles along an indoor river, the game tells the story of Judy. Judy is a film star who became famous for her beauty and talent, but one day her beauty begins to fade and her world turns dark. Broken down into chapters, you'll need to run, hide and stay away from Judy as she prowls the area. You're only equipped with a flashlight at first, so you'll need to use all your cunning and skills to stay safe.

WHAT MAKES A GREAT
PET SIMULATOR?

Roblox is full of games where you can adopt and raise pets, sometimes even evolving them into new creatures. In most of these games, you'll find familiar animals, but there are plenty of bizarre and wacky beasts too. Which pets have you collected so far?

ALL THE PETS

■ Have you always wanted to keep a tiger as a pet? Maybe an otter, or even a unicorn? If so, pet simulators are the games you should be playing. Many of the biggest pet sim games will have seasonal animals that come and go, allowing you to adopt them and build a HUGE collection of different creatures. It's not just familiar animals either, you can see mythological beasts such as griffins and the phoenix.

NEED IT!

■ Collecting all the different pets can be great fun, but what do you do with the doubles? Many of the pet sim games, such as Adopt Me! allow players to combine extras of certain animals to upgrade them. Often you can combine several fully grown animals to create a whole new version of them. These new animals are the rarest creatures as they take a long time to collect, grow and then combine them.

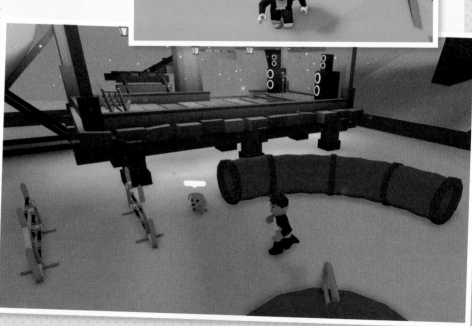

CARE AND RAISE

■ You won't just be hatching eggs and leaving the pets at home. Through feeding and playing, your pets will grow from babies into fully grown adults. Your pets are friends and companions who can explore the game worlds with you. Make sure they're happy, healthy and looking at their best as other players will want to meet your new best friend!

TIME TO TRADE

■ Thankfully many of these pet simulators allow players to trade their pets with each other; perfect for when you need just one more creature for your neon trade! Players can chat to each other and swap pets, building bigger collections – very helpful if you missed some seasonal animals or can't get the buddy you need from hatching eggs.

PLAYTIME

■ It's not just about pets (though it's mostly about pets, of course), many of these sims have mini-games you can play either with friends or with your little buddies. And many of these games will help you bond with your pet, allowing them to grow big and strong. Or you can win games to earn in-game money, which can be spent on clothes and accessories for your favourite pet.

TIPS AND TRICKS

● Collecting pets in any pet simulator is very simple. The first step is to find the shop that sells pet eggs and grab your first egg. Normally this first egg is free, whereas others will cost either money earned in the game, or real money.

● Your first egg will also likely only hatch a common pet. This means that the animal will be one that many people already have in their collection. However, different eggs can hatch much rarer animals.

● You may find that the pet simulator you've chosen to play requires you to explore the world with the egg bouncing along behind your avatar. Others may have a nest in a house you can decorate, while another may ask you to fight or play mini-games with your egg by your side before it hatches.

● If you love collecting, you may find that some pets never seem to hatch for you. If this is the case, then you may need to trade with other players. Before you trade with anyone, see if you have any friends who play the same game as you and may have the pet you need, instead of approaching a player you don't know.

● Most pet simulators feature different seasons where they introduce new animals – sea life, desert, mythological and much more. These seasons will normally feature not just new animals, but also very rare versions of the animals on offer. It's around these times you will find many more people playing than normal.

GREAT PET SIMULATORS

So you know what to expect from a pet simulator now, which ones should you play? This selection of games combines all the elements we've looked at with dozens of furry (and slimy and scaly) animal friends.

PET SIMULATOR X!

▓ Pet Simulator X! has slowly grown into one of the most popular games on Roblox. Why? Because it's so easy to pick up and play. Beginning with one of three basic pets, you will be able to explore the starting area, which is full of stacks of coins that your pet can collect for you. Once you've gained a nice stash of money, you can buy an egg to hatch. Your new egg will hatch straight away and reward you with a new pet.

▓ At first you can only equip four pets, but don't worry, this number will grow over time. The more pets you have, the faster you can harvest the gold coins, and the more coins you have, the more things you can do. For example, you can unlock new areas, which have larger stacks of coins and give new themed eggs to hatch.

76.86k

Make Golden Pets!

▓ Like other pet simulators, you're able to combine your pets to get a better, rarer pet. Here you can combine four of the same animal to create a golden version. If you struggle to hatch the right animals, you can trade with friends or other players to boost your collection.

▓ There are also plenty of themed events that offer limited-edition pets and lots of fantasy animals, which will make your group stand out to others.

ADOPT ME!

Adopt Me! is still one of the most popular games on Roblox. Why? Because it was one of the first pet simulators that let players collect and trade so many animals. Players fell in love with being able to create neon and mega-neon pets by combining their extra animals.

As pets come in several rarities, it can be tough to build a full collection, but hatching eggs is a big part of what makes the collecting so fun. Adopt Me! also allows players to use potions to change their pets into rideable, or even flying, creatures that can be used to explore the world!

PET SWARM SIMULATOR

This pet simulator focuses on using your pets to fight for you. When you spawn into the world, you'll have to hatch three eggs that'll become your first pets. You can then use your pets to fight enemies. These baddies all drop a type of egg that can be planted in your nest. Hatching these new eggs is as simple as harvesting fruit and feeding it to the eggs. Soon you'll have a little swarm of pets that can be upgraded by combining extras together, then it will be time to travel to new, distant lands for bigger and better battling pets.

BEE SWARM SIMULATOR

Have you ever wanted to be a beekeeper? It feels like a very calming hobby – caring for bees that collect pollen and transform it into honey. That's exactly what you do here! You'll need to build up a swarm of bees, guide them to flowers and collect the honey they make. This can be sold for cash that you can then use to hatch more bees or improve their productivity. You can even dress up your bee friends and make them look all fancy!

ZOMBIES EVERYWHERE!

Zombies have always been scary. Whether they trundle along or sprint like an Olympian, they feel dangerous. No matter how many times we kill them, they keep coming back for more! Let's look at some of the best zombie games on Roblox and aim for the head.

PROJECT LAZARUS

Project Lazarus is a hardcore shooter game, where working together as a team is VERY important. This is not an easy game to play solo. Waves of zombies will approach the building you must defend, and they are not easy to kill! You'll need to block off windows and doors to keep them out. They can break through over time, so your defences must be repaired once you've taken down the intruding zombies. With lots of weapons to choose from, you can easily find a favourite and upgrade it over time gradually.

FIELD TRIP Z

While there is plenty of fighting in Field Trip Z, it takes a little while to get there. There's a good chunk of story to play through at the beginning, which is great fun. With a large high school to explore with other players, you'll need to block up windows, grab weapons and fight to survive. It's not just waves of zombies, though, there are some HUGE enemies to battle too. And between fights, jumping on a wheely chair and zooming around corridors is just as fun as it can be in real life.

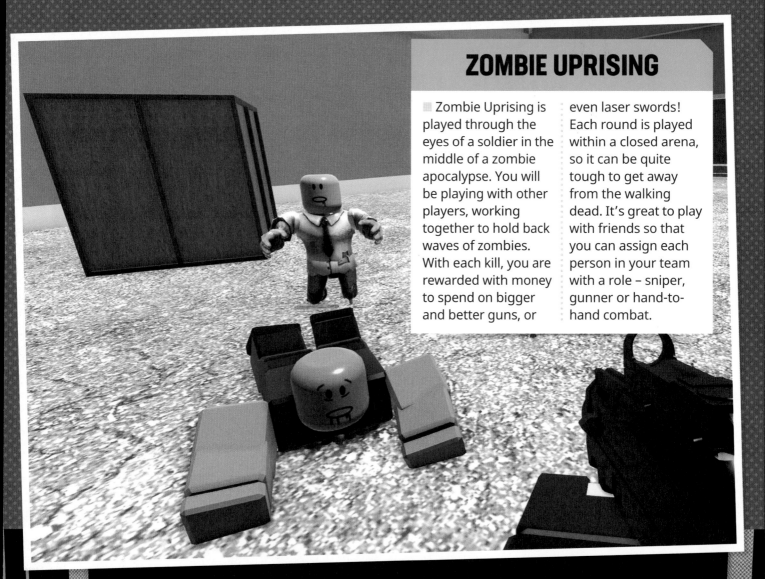

ZOMBIE UPRISING

Zombie Uprising is played through the eyes of a soldier in the middle of a zombie apocalypse. You will be playing with other players, working together to hold back waves of zombies. With each kill, you are rewarded with money to spend on bigger and better guns, or even laser swords! Each round is played within a closed arena, so it can be quite tough to get away from the walking dead. It's great to play with friends so that you can assign each person in your team with a role – sniper, gunner or hand-to-hand combat.

ZOMBIE ATTACK

Much like the other games on this list, the zombies in this game are battled in waves. Once one wave is eliminated, the other invades and you must destroy them all. Zombie Attack is played in third-person perspective, which means the camera is up behind your avatar. Playing on a team of others, each kill rewards you with funds to spend on new weapons as you defend a small town. The areas here are much bigger, so you can find some great places to sit and defend or just roam around, taking out any zombies you find.

WHAT MAKES A GREAT
OBBY?

An obby is an obstacle course, where you race to the end of increasingly difficult levels. There are so many great obbys; some require you to play fast, others are ultra-difficult and need a lot of skill to complete. But there are some things that all awesome obbys have in common.

GREAT ENVIRONMENTS

■ Some obbys are big, bright rainbows – obstacles in eye-popping colours. These are fun but can get a bit boring quickly. It's much better to have an area that has a particular theme. This helps make the obby a lot more interesting. It could be a simple jail, or a killer funfair. Finding a great obby usually means your avatar will be escaping from somewhere, and some games offer a little story while you make your way out too.

CHECK OUT:
Escape Prison Obby

CHECK OUT:
Escape Inflatable Obby

OBSTACLES

■ Beware of obstacles – that's where the name comes from after all. It's good for these to start off simple before building up to challenges, and there are lots of ways to do this. You'll have to balance on narrow walkways, jump long distances onto tiny platforms and drop through dangers that will reset your character if touched. Some of the more difficult obby games will have spinning platforms, moving ledges or small gaps to jump through. Thankfully many obbys have checkpoints between obstacles, just in case.

TRAPS

■ Traps come in all shapes and sizes from puddles of acid, which cause your player to crumble into pieces when touched, or giant sawblades that'll cause more than a scratch. They all contribute to a sense of real danger throughout levels. We love spikes springing out of the ceilings, swinging balls that must be dodged, jets of flames blasting from walls, endless drops or giant pools of bubbling lava.

CHECK OUT:
Escape the Carnival

CHECK OUT:
Tower of Hell

INCREASING DIFFICULTY

■ Some obbys will only come in one difficulty. Some are designed to be nice and easy – a good place to start when you want to learn how to play an obby. While some are beastly and tough (a few of these don't even have checkpoints) and they'll truly test your skills. A few obbys will have different paths through to the end, with each being rated with different difficulties. It's good to start off slow and learn how to control your avatar while it's moving, noting how far and high they can jump.

SKILLS

■ Some obbys have abilities that change the way you can navigate levels. Some sections will need to be beaten after you've been given a super-speed boost; or your jump may be stronger, allowing you to go higher or further. You might even find a level where the gravity is lower and your avatar floats around making the jumps a little easier. These abilities can be great, but they may also make the obby much harder. Explore and find the levels you enjoy the most.

CHECK OUT:
Escape the Dungeon

IT'S MAGIC!

Many of the games within Roblox can turn you into a movie star, wizard, superhero, or even a powerful villain. Roblox gives you a chance to live out a fantasy life you could never have outside of the game. Which kind of superstar will you be?

WACKY WIZARDS

In Wacky Wizards you play the role of a young wizard who is trying to become a master mage. The starting area features low-level enemies who can be beaten with ease. The only downside is your wizard can't hold much magic power at first. This needs to be upgraded by beating more enemies. As you progress, enemies get bigger and scarier until they feel unbeatable – thankfully you'll learn many more spells and even recruit a pet, which can help with the fights. Wacky Wizards feels like a very deep and large RPG. It starts off a little slow, but soon you'll find yourself playing for hours as you search out those dangerous bosses!

SUPER POWER FIGHTING SIMULATOR

Becoming the ultimate superhero takes a long time. Plenty of training, brawling with small enemies and pesky low-level bosses. What you never really see are the long days of push-ups or sparring. Through all these small tasks, your weakling hero will begin gaining strength, speed and a higher health bar. Only then can you head out and start stomping on those big bosses and maniac villains. As you fight and keep the streets safe, you'll earn money to change your hero outfit and you may find chests to open, which contain valuable items. There are even massive swords and shields for you to use!

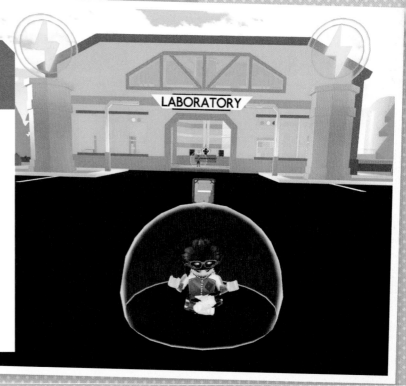

LEGENDS OF SPEED

Have you ever wanted to run so fast that you become a blur? It takes a lot of work, but you can get there by racing others in this game. At first, you'll be jogging around picking up small items, which will reward you with XP to help you level up. As each level passes you get faster and are soon zooming all over the place! Eventually you'll be leaping through reward hoops or beating opponents to get even faster. Reaching the highest levels, you will become that blur and people's mouths will drop to the floor at your speed.

WIZARD SIMULATOR

It sounds simple, but in Wizard Simulator, the idea is to pretend to be a wizard. This is done by exploring the area for potion ingredients and then mixing them together before drinking your potion and finding out what it does. It might make your avatar HUGE or tiny. A potion may give you noodle arms or turn you into a toy. There are some enemies in this simulator, but as there are other players are in the arena with you, you could ignore the bosses and just keep mixing funny potions.

PvP

Roblox is known for community. While many of the games can be played alone, so many of them are better played with others. However, if you don't want to team up with your friends and prefer to play competitively, there are plenty of options for PvP (player vs player).

SHOOTERS

■ Shooting games are generally known for pitting players against each other. It may be in a team deathmatch-style or gather many players to see who can hit the target eliminations fastest. And of course, there are Battle Royales. However you prefer to play, there's a shooter on Roblox for you. It's worth trying out a few as they vary in style. These games can be simple, with only a few weapons, or more complex, with lots of guns that react to the physics of the world.

RACING

■ Racing games tend to come in two types on Roblox – structured racing and open exploration. The first brings players together, places them on a track and requires you to complete a set number of laps. The second sees you driving around a city, challenging random players or even completing stunts to see who can score the most points.

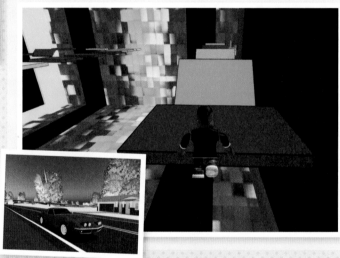

MINI-GAMES

■ There are several mini-game collections to find on Roblox. They tend to mimic other games or even challenge players to more hardcore versions of playground classics. These PvP games tend to be casual and fun, rather than intense, which you may find with a shooter. Expect bright and colourful games with a party atmosphere.

BIG! PAINTBALL

BIG! Paintball feels more like an arcade game – it's bold and colourful, but most importantly, it's fun! The weapons copy those from the real world but shoot paintballs at your opponents, leaving them as a bright splatter. With lots of weapons to choose from, you can slot yourself into a role on your team. Maybe you like to sit back and snipe? Or do you prefer to get in close and keep moving? Whichever weapon you favour, it will feel great in your hands.

RAGE RUNNER

Rage Runner isn't a shooting game, but you still play against others to see who will win each game. So if you're not fighting, what are you doing? Well, running. Fast. Each round of the game generates a random course where you need to reach the end before anyone else. It sounds simple, but your avatar runs VERY quickly, and your jumps and movements must be accurate. It gets even harder when other players grab power-ups, which can completely change how the game plays.

POLYBATTLE

Using a 'low-poly' form of graphics, Polybattle ignores good graphics for great gameplay. Played through the eyes of your avatar, you must eliminate other players and capture certain sections of the map to score points for your team. There are so many guns to use, and the shooting always feels accurate and powerful. Matches don't last too long, so you can get plenty of games in. Try linking up with your friends and build a powerful and unstoppable squad!

38 MPH

TURRET

PvP MASTERCLASS

What does it look like when you combine all the elements that make a great PvP game into one single game? Simple; Bed Wars. This legendary Roblox game is a shining example of what creators can achieve when they aim to make the best PvP game they can.

BED WARS

The objective of Bed Wars is to destroy your opponents' beds, which are found on their individual starting islands. Beds can be destroyed any number of ways and it's up to you to defend your bed by either fighting those invading your island or by using blocks to build a shield around the bed. The blocks can be broken by anyone, but it will slow people down and keep them at a safe distance from you.

You'll start with a sword and a pickaxe and the ability to build with coloured blocks. As the rounds progress, you'll earn currency to buy better swords and even armour to keep you alive for longer. Your pickaxe is an important tool for breaking the blocks of other players, plus it can destroy their bed.

As the starting islands are set apart from each other, and with a long drop to death below, you'll need to use your blocks. Blocks can be used to build bridges, climb to high points or to form walls around your bed.

● Balance playing offensively and defensively, especially if you're playing solo. While you may want to rush in and destroy an opponent's bed, you must make sure yours is safe too. If you play on a team, talk to your teammates and decide who will defend and who will attack.

● You can collect iron bars from inside your base. Diamonds and emeralds are found on the far edges of the map. You use these to gain better swords or legendary weapons. Try to mine blocks when you're not fighting and find those resources!

● Watch your enemies constantly. If you see them moving towards your bed, rush back and prepare to defend. Try to knock them off the edge of the map or box them in for a close-quarters elimination.

● Learn all the items and weapons. TNT blocks, for example, are valuable and can change the tide of a match, but you need to be aware of how long they take to explode.

● Don't just rush in for the fight. You can use the opening moments to find resources and gear up properly. Rushing in can often leave you eliminated early, especially to talented players who will use advanced tactics against you.

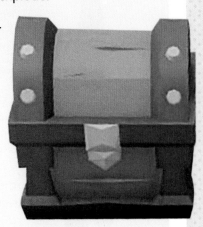

AVATAR WARDROBE
CHARACTERS

On Roblox, you can be whoever you want to be. One of the ways to define your personality on the platform is to change the way your avatar looks. These characters are all wildly different, but there's one for every kind of game!

JESTER EQUINOX

■ With a clever vertically-split costume design, the Jester Equinox character perfectly typifies the balance of light and dark, of night and day. Embellished with moons and suns, and sporting a cheerful happy expression, it's a skin that will bring a smile to any who see it.

THE GNOMSKY BROTHERS

■ Why dress up as one character when you can dress up as two instead? These mischievous gnome brothers stack themselves to reach the height of a normal Robloxian, so they can try to blend in with the regular folk. But you'll spot this funny pair a mile away! Now if only they could invest in a long raincoat to cover one of their faces, they might have more success!

UD'ZAL

■ This spooky Korbloxian is the 'all-father' of the evil Korblox race. Or at least he was until he was killed and revived by a group of Deathspeakers. The spooky torso face will send shivers down the spine of your fellow Robloxians.

TENKO THE NINE-TAILED FOX

■ You'll definitely be able to see Tenko coming from afar – those nine bushy foxtails are huge! This Japanese-inspired character is said to be able to alter its appearance and age with a magical mask, perfect for those who like a change.

DJ DATABAZE

■ It's time to party! This dazzling techno DJ loves nothing more than dancing to the beats blasting from her kitten-ear headphones. In fact, she looks a bit like a kitten, with furry sleeves, socks and skirt to boot. She even has a long feline tail! You can find her at the wheels of steel in all of the hottest parties around Robloxia. Ask nicely and maybe she'll play at yours!

BLOCKY MECH

■ The bulky, blue armour shines in the light as Blocky Mech swoops into action. With pneumatic arms, pinpoint vision and an arsenal of deadly missiles on its back, it's certainly a character that will strike fear into enemy combatants.

KARA LYE

■ One part sky pirate, one part demon, Kara Lye is wholly fearsome. She's a terror of the skies, who cuts a path through the highest clouds and keeps her eagle eyes out for ships carrying valuable loot. She can swoop through the skies on her devilish wings and strike at her enemies with her glistening Rapier of Fury, Trinity. They'll never see her coming from above!

DON'T GET SCARED

Horror games are some of the most popular on Roblox. We all like to be a little bit scared from time to time. But which terrifying games do you choose to play when there are so many? We've got you covered with some of our spooky favourites.

SPIDER

SPIDER is a hunting game, where survivors must hide and escape the player who has been given the role of spider. The spider is very creepy; a Roblox avatar bent over into itself and crawling on all fours. Not only is it creepy, but it's fast! As a survivor, you will need to work with other players to unlock doors, find items and escape the area before the spider grabs you and eliminates you. SPIDER is still rather new, so there aren't many maps yet, but hopefully we'll be able to run away screaming in terror on new maps soon enough.

THE MIMIC

This game is more story-based than the others on the list. It's also inspired by Japanese urban legends and ghost stories. It's your job to follow clues and work through the story while staying safe. It's great to read the in-game notes about the ghosts and then find them chasing you. Did we mention that Japanese ghost stories are among the scariest in the world?! They are, so be prepared to get scared, creeped out and terrified.

SPECTER

This game is brilliant to play with your friends, preferably over voice chat. Specter is genuinely scary! You and a small group will be given the role of ghost inspectors. Armed with torches and basic items in the game worlds, you need to track and trace plenty of ghosts and ghoulies. Expect plenty of darkness and jump scares (hearing your friends scream or yell is often very funny). Specter is a very intense game, which will give you nightmares for days to come!

PIGGY

As one of the most popular horror games on Roblox, you've probably already played PIGGY. Or maybe you know somebody who keeps telling you to try it. We're here to give you a nudge in that direction too. Broken down into chapters, this survival horror has a strong story running through it. The game itself is like others, in that players enter the game, and one is chosen to be PIGGY. It's their job to eliminate all the other players who are trying to survive. With over twenty maps to play, lots of items to use and a few different game modes to try, PIGGY has so much content to play through and keep you busy. Plus it's super scary!

HIDDEN GEMS

OUTLASTER

▨ Outlaster feels like a TV show; players gather together in a lobby before being split into two teams under captains. From this point, the idea is to take your team to victory by working together in the mini-games and obstacle courses. The key here is that after each round a player will be voted off the team, so you must work with others and do your very best if you don't want to be voted off by your teammates. With all the different games and the team chat and voting in between, Outlaster is a great game to play with a group of friends.

VEHICLE LEGENDS

▨ There are a lot of driving games on Roblox. Some are based on races; others ask you to explore. Vehicle Legends does both and does them very well. You start with a basic, but great, car to drive right away. Driving around the world, you'll be rewarded with money when you discover new locations or win mini-races against other players. It doesn't take long to round up enough cash to buy a new car, bike, or even plane. The most important thing about any racing game is how the vehicles feel while playing, and whether you're on a controller, keyboard or touch screen, this game feels great to drive around in.

AQUALINA WATER PARK

A water park you can play in even if it's raining? Count us in! In Aqualina life is simple, all you need to do is show up with some friends and ride the water slides. There are plenty of pools and the slides come in all sizes and styles. This game isn't overloaded with shops, items and power-ups; there's a shop to buy accessories and outfits, but everything can be experienced without these things (though it might be best to buy a swimsuit!). Jump in, the water is great!

TREASURE QUEST

Do you like fighting bad guys and collecting treasure? We do too. That is exactly what happens in Treasure Quest; you'll start off with a sword and you need to push on through the dungeon through LOTS of enemies! With each room cleared, chests can be opened that are bursting with gold coins and these coins can be used to buy new equipment in order to take on tougher dungeons. But you'll also find weapons in the chests, which makes you want to fight everyone, explore everything and defeat the huge bosses at the end of each dungeon. A great game to play on your own, but perfect with a few friends.

MY DRAGON TYCOON

Dragons are cool, there's no doubting that. They're even better when you can fight alongside one. In My Dragon Tycoon, your job is to make money and fight lots of enemies with your scaly pal. Starting with a basic sword and a dragon egg, you'll have to build a factory to mine gems, and fight easy enemies to earn money. Once you've got both, you'll be able to upgrade your factory and equipment, and hatch your dragon, who will help you fight, run the factory and battle others. You can even face off against other dragon tycoons if you want to prove that you're the best in the world.

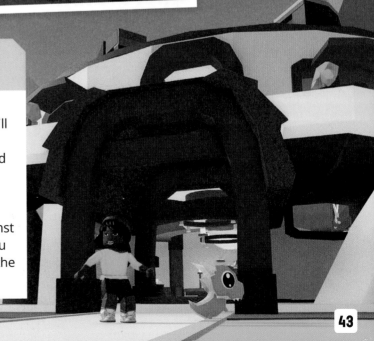

PETS

If you can't get enough of playing with pets in games, or becoming an animal for that matter, then you can customise your avatar with a pet pal so that you're never without a furry friend. Let's take a look at a few of the best.

CUTE WANDERING GHOST

■ This shy little guy peeks out from behind your legs as if it's a little nervous. But with blushing cheeks and a bright smile, it shouldn't be afraid to make some new friends. There's nothing scary about this friendly little spectre either.

CHRISTMAS SNOWMAN BUDDY

■ Measuring almost as tall as an avatar, it's hard to really call this snowman a pet. But the frosty friend will follow you wherever you go. It has the classic coal, carrot and stick decorations, as well as a cosy hat and scarf to keep it warm. But not too warm or it'll melt.

PLUSHY CHIBI PANDA

■ If you're willing to give your pet a piggyback, this friendly panda is perfect. It will sit on your shoulders as you walk around, munching on its favourite bamboo shoots. Sure, it's a little bit lazy – aren't we all – but it makes up for it with unbearable cuteness. Aw!

OVERSEER OVERSLEEPER: TERRIBLE TEDDY

■ Cute animals aren't to everyone's taste, so if you prefer your pet pal to have a bit of a dark side, this ominous teddy might do the trick. Supposedly cuddled up to by the evil Korbloxian Overseers, this cyclopic bear is perfect when you're in a squeeze.

CAT SHOULDER PAL

■ Show your love for the first massive in-game pet, the Huge Cat. This replica resembles it in every way... but is a fraction of the size! It's small enough to sit on your shoulder, but it's big eyes and ears will keep guard of the situation around you to keep you safe at all times.

HAPPY NEW YEAR RAT

■ Kick off the Chinese New Year with a bang with this cute little critter, adorned in red and gold. He'll scamper up onto your shoulder and bring you fortune as you make your way through Robloxia. He could come in handy for some tycoon games!

KAWAII PINK OCTOPUS

■ With its ginormous eyes and short stubby tentacles, this adorable creature makes the perfect cuddly companion on your travels. It will sit on your head like a hat, where its happy face will beam down at anyone you meet.

PEACEFUL PLAYING

Sometimes you don't want to play a game full of action, weapons and a high skill level. You might want something a little more chill or relaxing. There are plenty of options within Roblox and many of them give you a chance to take a well-needed break.

STEPFORD COUNTY RAILWAY

▓ Stepford County Railway is probably the most intricate and in-depth vehicle game on Roblox. You can play as one of several roles, which all offer different types of gameplay. Of course, it's likely you'll mostly want to drive the train though. This game is best played on a keyboard as there are many buttons set to the functions of the train. It's not just moving back and forth along the tracks; you'll need to stick to speed limits, open doors for passengers and make sure you don't run late!

MATH OBBY

▓ Math Obby starts off nice and easy, adding small numbers to each other, before growing in difficulty. Between maths problems are small obby sections, some of which can be quite tricky to navigate. As you approach the end of the obby, there will be a maths question to solve. You'll need to work out each answer before powering through the answer door to move on to the next section of the obby. There are no punishments for the wrong answer, you simply won't progress. Some of the later levels will really test your brain, and your skills.

HIDE AND SEEK EXTREME

We're not entirely sure what makes this version of Hide and Seek so extreme. Maybe it's because the seeker has special abilities, or it might be because the players have been shrunk, making each map HUGE. Each round of this classic game lasts only a few minutes, so you can move quickly from one game to another. If you're hiding, choose a great place, but remember you can move freely. As the seeker, you'll need to use your ability to help you find everyone before the time runs out.

EXPEDITION ANTARCTICA

This chilly game is an obby in an exploration disguise. When you first spawn into the game, you will need to collect your equipment and safety gear. From here you can practise moving around on the slippery ice, or head straight out into the wilds of Antarctica. Your goal is the South Pole. While progress feels like an obby – narrow platforms, platform jumping, etc. – you also need to keep an eye on your character's energy levels and how cold they are. Ignore these and you will find your character dies from exposure to the environment.

WEIRD AND WONDERFUL

Roblox is full of weird and wonderful games – it's a great place for developers to let their imaginations run wild. If you can think of it, someone has probably made a game about it. So, let's take a look at the weirder side of Roblox.

SHARKBITE

There are lots of games where one person plays as a killer or hunter, while others try to survive. With this one, there's a slight difference – the hunter is a shark. Yep, you read that right; you can play as a shark, swimming through the waters looking for people to gobble up. Can you eat all the survivors before they manage to hunt you?

BUILD A BOAT TO SURVIVE

In this game, you must build a boat using different blocks of various shapes. Starting in a small grassy workshop area, you have a little gold that you must spend on your boat's building blocks. Once you've spent your budget, press a button to launch the boat down a river full of obstacles. The further your boat gets, the more money you earn, which can then be spent on more blocks next time. How far can you get your boat?

SUPER BOMB SURVIVAL

As you enter the arena in Super Bomb Survival, you'll be joined by lots of other players. The aim of the game? To stay alive for as long as possible while bombs fall from the sky in random places. As the bombs drop, the arena will be blown to bits! It takes a lot of tactics and a little bit of luck to survive. Plus you can take advantage of the power-ups that appear and could grant you a super jump, a shield or other bonkers abilities.

LITTLE WORLD

You start Little World as a tiny ladybird. If you explore the world – where you can buy houses and pets – you'll find fruit to be collected. Picking up these juicy snacks will level up your bug, slowly evolving it into new types of insects. This all happens in between rounds of mini-games or big boss battles, which reward you with gems to be spent on accessories. The mini-games are great fun and are all very different and exciting!

BUBBLE GUM SIMULATOR

What if you could sell the bubbles you blow? That's the idea here – chew the gum, blow the biggest bubble you can and then sell that bubble (who is buying these bubbles?!) for gold. You can use this gold to buy better gum, which means you can blow bigger bubbles and earn more money. You can even change the colour or pattern of the gum. Odd, but interesting.

AVATAR WARDROBE
ACCESSORIES

||||||||||||||||||||||||||||||||||||||||||||||||||||||||||||||||||||||||||||||||||||||||||||||||||||||||||||

An outfit isn't complete until you accessorise! Luckily, Roblox has virtual shelves full of accessories, from headphones and hats to jewellery and weapons. Let's take a look at some of the best that the store has to offer.

COLD STARE SKATEBOARD

■ Always be ready to shred the tarmac with this awesome skateboard that you wear on your back. The design on the bottom is of a pair of eerie eyes so that you can always watch what's going on behind you when you're not pulling off rad tricks.

BASICALLY I'M BABY

■ If you're a big fan of games like Adopt Me, where you can raise a family and make a happy home, then this clever accessory is perfect. It's a baby carrier, complete with a baby noob that you can take with you.

INSTANT CAMERA

■ Get snap-happy with this trendy instant camera that you wear around your neck. Whether you're scrapbooking memories or taking pictures of your latest tasty meal, this will print instant memories whenever you click the button.

STYROFOAM COMPANION

■ If the aim of your outfit is to shock people rather than impress them, then there's really only one option: the Styrofoam Companion. The creepy construction has rudimentary hair, eyes and lips and protrudes from your shoulder. It'll send shivers down many a spine.

BEAR FACE MASK

■ Unfortunately due to the pandemic, masks have become ever more common around the world. But that doesn't mean they can't be stylish too! This bear-themed mask will hide your expression behind an indifferent bear mouth instead.

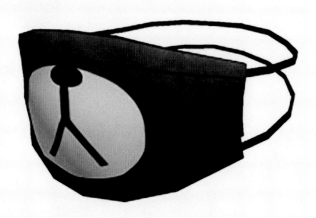

PRIDE CROSSBODY BAG

■ Celebrate love in all its forms with the Pride Crossbody Bag. The transparent bag is emblazoned with the rainbow flag to represent solidarity with the LGBTQ+ community. And just as importantly, it will look great sashed across your outfit too.

FLAMINGO FLOATY

■ Safety is important, especially around rivers, lakes and oceans. Take no chances with the water or your style by wearing the Flamingo Floaty everywhere you go. Not only will you look like a showy bird, you'll also stop yourself drowning too!

PEACEFUL PLAYING

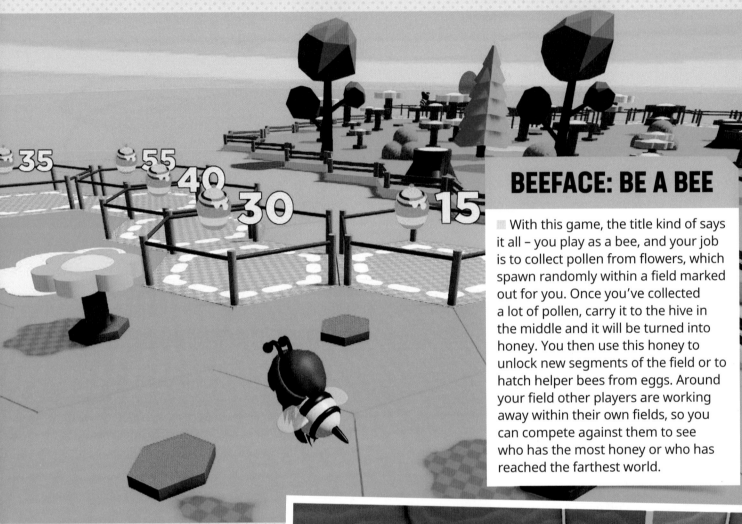

BEEFACE: BE A BEE

With this game, the title kind of says it all – you play as a bee, and your job is to collect pollen from flowers, which spawn randomly within a field marked out for you. Once you've collected a lot of pollen, carry it to the hive in the middle and it will be turned into honey. You then use this honey to unlock new segments of the field or to hatch helper bees from eggs. Around your field other players are working away within their own fields, so you can compete against them to see who has the most honey or who has reached the farthest world.

TREASURE HUNT SIMULATOR

In this treasure hunt, all you need to worry about is digging for treasure chests. Starting with a tiny bucket and backpack, you dig away at blocks of sand. When your backpack is full, a nearby shop buys the sand. Then you can use the money to buy bigger tools and backpacks, which speeds up the process. Finding a chest is always great – they span from common wooden chests up to ultra-rare rainbow versions. Each chest holds a bit more money to spend. It's great fun to explore deeper as the blocks go down for hundreds of layers, but of course, chests become harder to find and take longer to dig out.

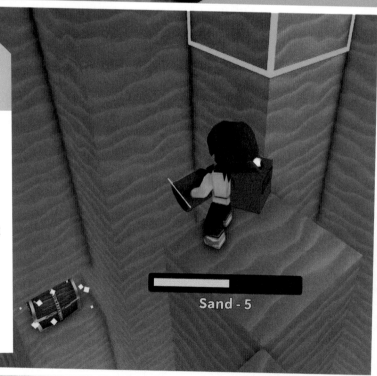

Sand - 5

PAINT SIMULATOR

▦ In Paint Simulator, you take on the role of a painter. Filling the paint pod strapped to your back, you must wander around the playing area spreading colour and patterns on walls and canvasses. Over time, you'll earn money for your painting, which can be spent on bigger paint pods and will unlock new areas to explore. The best part of Paint Simulator is the artwork, most of which is inspired by real-world art, so you'll get to see some beautiful masterpieces while you roam the world.

BUILD IT

▦ The goal of Build It is a simple one. Several players enter an arena and are given a topic. Then, using blocks of various colours, you must build something related to the topic you've been given. After a set amount of time has run out, everyone's building will be revealed and then voting can start on who built the best sculpture related to the theme. Build It is a wonderful, creative game that can be played with friends or complete strangers.

IT'S CALLED PHYSICS

Roblox is famous for its physics engine. But what is it? Essentially, it's code that emulates natural forces like gravity. When you blow up a building and bricks fly everywhere? That's the physics engine at work! Some creators have put physics at the heart of their experiences. Let's take a look!

NATURAL DISASTER SURVIVAL

The idea behind Natural Disaster Survival is to stay alive however you can. You'll enter an area with a bunch of other players and suddenly an alarm will ring telling you a disaster is coming. It could be fire, a cyclone or an earthquake. Whichever it is, you need to hide or run and dodge the destruction as buildings crumble and even the ground begins to break open then fall away. Watch for lights, ceilings and support beams tumbling down and knocking you out.

DESTRUCTION PHYSICS

Destruction Physics could be a great way to unwind after a long day. Ultimately the game gives you an area or a building, along with tools and items to destroy the area fully. Walls crumble, windows shatter and smash, chunks of bricks fly outward to who knows where! A great game to play with friends as a small group of you run around with sledgehammers busting and breaking everything in sight. It's quite relaxing, really.

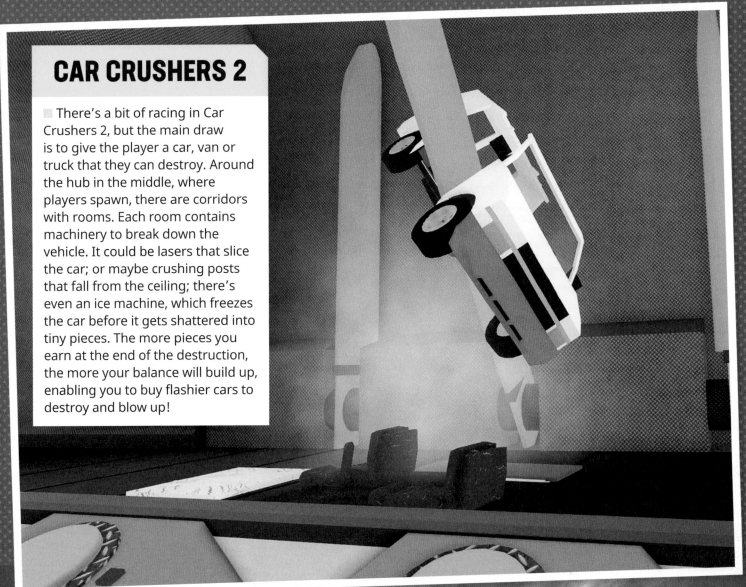

CAR CRUSHERS 2

There's a bit of racing in Car Crushers 2, but the main draw is to give the player a car, van or truck that they can destroy. Around the hub in the middle, where players spawn, there are corridors with rooms. Each room contains machinery to break down the vehicle. It could be lasers that slice the car; or maybe crushing posts that fall from the ceiling; there's even an ice machine, which freezes the car before it gets shattered into tiny pieces. The more pieces you earn at the end of the destruction, the more your balance will build up, enabling you to buy flashier cars to destroy and blow up!

RAGDOLL SIMULATOR

Ragdoll Simulator is a large playground where you can torment and antagonise your avatar, making them flail their arms and legs. There are so many ways to launch, squash or yeet them. You might use a cannon; or push them down hundreds of stairs; sit them in front of a spinning hammer, or take them to the bouncy room. We're sure these acts break every bone in their bodies, but with a button press, they're back to normal, strolling around and towards the next painful collapse.

IS THIS A SIMULATION?

You may have noticed there are A LOT of simulator games on Roblox. No matter what you're interested in, there will be a simulator for you, so give them all a try. You might find an exciting game based on something that may not look incredible at first glance.

FACTORY SIMULATOR

Factory Simulator is a management game that lets you design and build an automated factory. Initially you'll chop down trees or smash rocks and dump these into a box. The box is connected to a conveyer belt that deposits the materials into a selling zone. Anything that enters the 'sell zone' earns you money. Using these funds, you can buy more automated equipment such as a sawmill to chop the wood, or a press to compact materials. These altered items earn more money and after some time, you'll have a huge factory full of conveyer belts and stations, which process and deliver the materials you're collecting outside. It's a very satisfying game as you can watch your raw materials pass through stations before being sold for big bucks!

STRONGMAN SIMULATOR

The title of this simulator may give away the goal of the game. At first, your avatar is tiny and skinny. Your first job is to earn energy, which can then be spent at the exercise area. As you're so small, all you'll be able to do is drag feathers across a short course. Once you've built some strength, you can drag large rubber ducks or toilets (yes, toilets!). Eventually your avatar will grow and develop huge muscles. New areas will unlock and you'll grow to be the size of a tall building with bulging muscles popping out everywhere!

BUILD TO SURVIVE SIMULATOR

Every couple of minutes a disaster is going to occur. It could be a giant crocodile roaming the arena, or a sudden flood of lava. Your mission is to stay alive by building suitable shelters using blocks of different materials. For example, if you know a lake of lava is going to flood your area, you'll want to build a platform above the area, so you don't get burned. If a giant killer doll is going to rampage through the area, you might build a brick cube to hide inside. This is a great game to play with friends to see how they each deal with the oncoming danger!

3-2-1 BLAST OFF SIMULATOR

Have you ever wanted to be an astronaut? You can live out that dream with this simulator. Although we're not too sure about the health and safety rules, as to ride the rocket, you must strap yourself onto the OUTSIDE of it! So what's the goal here? Collect lots of fuel, funnel it into your rocket and then launch it. You'll earn money for the journey – more money will be earned based on the height the rocket reaches. More fuel = more height = more money. At first, you'll be vacuuming the fuel by hand, but once the money pours in, you can operate drones that will collect fuel and leave you more time to ride the rocket to space!

THE MOST WANTED
COLLECTIBLES

There are some avatar items on Roblox that are only released in limited quantities, which tend to sell for thousands of Robux. If you're lucky, you'll be able to get your hands on one while they're still cheap, but for everyone else, we've compiled a showcase of the coolest on offer!

ST PATRICK'S DAY FAIRY

■ Channel the luck of the Irish with your own personal St Patrick's Day Fairy. The emerald-winged angel is adorned with gold decorations and surround by green sparkles that show her magic is working. She'll sit atop your shoulder, so you can keep your hands free too!

EGG ON YOUR FACE

■ You can even customise your expression with collectibles. Ten thousand Egg On Your Face items were snapped up by Robloxians who thought they'd look better with fried eggs for eyes. There's no accounting for taste ...

FIERY HORNS OF THE NETHERWORLD

■ If you think your avatar needs more of a fiery personality, then these exclusive horns are the perfect fit. Not only do they protrude prominently from the side of your head, they also create a fiery storm between them.

DOMINUS FRIGIDUS

■ One of a series of Dominus cowls, all of which are super expensive, the Dominus Frigidus headwear will obscure your face and make your look super mysterious. The cool icy blue colour makes it perfect to wear on chilly days too.

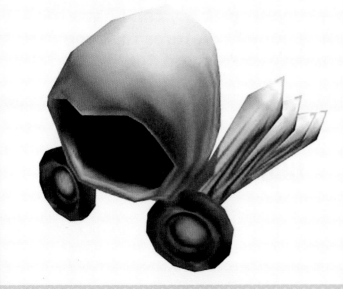

KUDDLE E. KOALA

■ If you prefer your headwear to be a little bit cuter and warmer, look no further than Kuddle E. Koala. The knitwear texture will keep your head toasty, while the ears, eyes and giant flat nose will remind everyone of their favourite tree-dwelling marsupial.

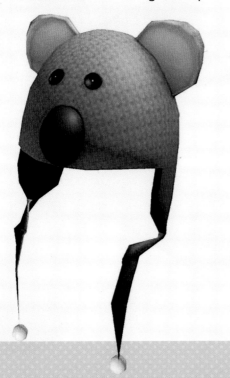

SKELEFRIEND

■ Having nobody to play with can be a drag, but this little skeleton friend has no body either – just bones! You'll carry this little fella around with you in any game you visit, so you always have a spooky pal to go on adventures with.

PURPLE SPARKLE TIME FEDORA

■ Some might think that the fedora is a boring hat for people of a certain age, but this glitzy purple version modernises the headwear for a whole new generation. If you're lucky enough to get your hands on one of only 100 versions, you'll be as stylish as anyone.

PETS

You can never have too many friends, and you certainly can't have too many animal friends. Here's another collection of creatures that you can get from the Avatar Shop to accompany you around Robloxia.

BABY DUCK FRIEND

■ Duck! Too late, a tiny duckling has landed on your head already. Luckily this cute baby duck is a friendly figure and it was just looking for somewhere to rest. And your head seems to make a nice roost. Unsurprisingly, it loves visiting the water and going on aquatic quests.

GIANT REINDEER FRIEND

■ The reindeer have finally had enough of taking Santa for a ride every Christmas, so now it's their turn to be carried everywhere. This massive reindeer will drape itself over your back like a humongous festive backpack. At least its bright red nose can be useful in the dark!

BAT BUDDY

■ Bats get a bad reputation for being spooky night creatures, but there's no mistaking the Bat Buddy as anything but adorable. Those giant friendly eyes and tiny little wings make it look like it's always asking for a hug!

MR. WHISKERS

■ Sure, you could pick a plain old cat to join you, but Mr. Whiskers has more personality in his tailbone than most other felines. This unique skelly loves nothing more than playing with you and his fish bones, which he's constantly chewing on.

MUSHROOM FRIEND (LEFT)

■ If you're looking for a fungi to hang around with then look no further than the Mushroom Friend. Your little toadstool buddy will stay by your side no matter what perils you lead it into, so it's a great pet to take with you wherever you go.

FLYING PINK AXOLOTL FRIEND

■ The axolotl is fast becoming one of the most popular animals on the planet, and looking at this little pink guy, it's easy to see why. The cute amphibian swims around your head, bringing joy to anyone who encounters it.

BEWITCHING AMPHIBIAN

■ If you can wear a hat, why can't your pets too? This funny little frog looks like an amphibious witch with its pointy hat and wild gaze. In fact, maybe it is a witch and one of her spells went wrong ... either way, it's a great pet to take along with you.

SPORTS TIME

Sports games allow us to keep playing games we love, even when the weather's awful. Here you can find some of the best sports games on Roblox, but if your favourite sport isn't listed, there's still a chance it exists anyway. And if it doesn't, why not create the game yourself?

SUPER GOLF!

▓ Super Golf! pits you against random players, or your friends to see who's the best at mini golf. The brilliance of this game comes from how simple it is. The controls are so easy to learn! Each course also looks wildly different and the holes get crazier as you progress – starting with simple straight-putting to later including loops and special sections that change how your ball moves. Can you beat all your friends?

FOOTBALL FUSION

▓ American Football can be a confusing sport to learn. Once mastered, it becomes a very intricate and wonderful game to play. Football Fusion allows you to take on any role from the team and play a match. The creators have managed to capture the beauty of the sport nicely. Playing as a Quarterback, you can make the ball spiral and glide through the air, while catching and running the ball to the end zone as a receiver feels more exciting and skillful. Give it a go yourself, even if football to you means not using your hands and kicking a sphere instead.

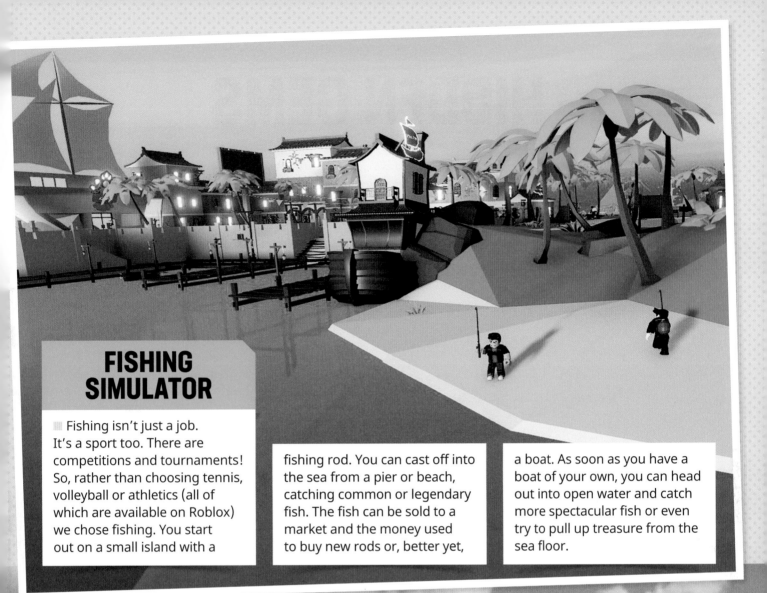

FISHING SIMULATOR

Fishing isn't just a job. It's a sport too. There are competitions and tournaments! So, rather than choosing tennis, volleyball or athletics (all of which are available on Roblox) we chose fishing. You start out on a small island with a fishing rod. You can cast off into the sea from a pier or beach, catching common or legendary fish. The fish can be sold to a market and the money used to buy new rods or, better yet, a boat. As soon as you have a boat of your own, you can head out into open water and catch more spectacular fish or even try to pull up treasure from the sea floor.

SPLASH: MUSIC & SKATE

SPLASH is the best skateboarding game on Roblox right now. It feels smooth as you speed down ramps or grind down rails. There are many tricks to pull off during the skating sessions, all of which rack up points against other players. Of course, you can customise your skateboard and your avatar, which adds another layer to the game. Interestingly, this game isn't just about skating, you can DJ the skating sessions or dance to the DJ sets too!

HIDDEN GEMS

CREATURES OF SONARIA

▓ This role-playing game plays a lot like an animal simulator; you choose a creature to play as and roam the world trying to survive. You'll have to monitor certain stats such as hunger, thirst and energy levels. This is important to keeping your creature alive and healthy. Of course, you'll end up getting into a fair few fights with other players and growing your monster will give you a better chance of winning these battles. The best part of Creatures of Sonaria is the number of creatures you can unlock and control. The designs are crazy and each creature behaves differently from the next. Try to find your favourite and survive the dangers of the world.

THE WILD WEST

▓ The Wild West is another role-playing game where your role depends on how you prefer to play. The world is massive and features plenty of activities for you and others. You could head into the hills and mine rocks for gems and minerals; play the criminal and rob banks. But if crime isn't your thing, then play as the sheriff and capture those sneaky thieves. The Wild West feels busy, with lots of players, animals to hunt and even an old steam train, which runs through the landscape. Many of these jobs and roles can be played alongside your friends, so will you choose the path of good or evil?

MERMAID LIFE

So many people would love to be a mermaid. Imagine it, drifting and swimming through the waves of the ocean, making friends with the fishes, living in coral houses. That's the idea here. Mermaid Life is a role-playing game where everyone is a fully customisable mermaid and can shop, play games or explore the underwater homes of other players. This is a game where you make the rules for life – go to lunch with your friends or collect cute fishy pets.

RANDOM RUMBLE

Random Rumble focuses on the randomiser genre of games where it seems as if anything could happen. Your primary task is to fight other players and eliminate as many people as possible. However, you will receive a completely random load-out. You have no control over which weapons you have, but this also extends to items and vehicles. For example, one round you might have a sword and a giant magnet, which pulls your opponents towards you. The next round, you might have a gun and a decoy which looks just like you but explodes in the enemy's face. It's bonkers fun!

CAMPING 2

Camping 2 is the follow-up to the popular Camping. It's a story-based adventure that is played with others, as you try to solve the mysteries of the campgrounds. At first, everything seems calm. It's just a regular camping trip in the woods. But before long, whittling up a fire is the least of your worries as disaster strikes, and the trip becomes a fight for survival. What is really going on? You'll have to play to find out!

RUN WILD AND FREE

There are so many games about adopting animals as pets, but what if you want to role-play as the animal instead? There are tons of games out there that are created to give you the best experience of 'being an animal'. Time to take a walk on the wild side.

WARRIOR CATS

One of the highlights of Warrior Cats has to be the character customisation. Before you get a chance to roam around the world, you must create a cat to play as. There are SO MANY options to choose from! You can choose colour, style of ears and tail, whether your cat has markings and even whether it will wear little shoes. Once your cat is ready to stretch their paws, it's time to start role-playing within the world. You'll be playing alongside other players and it's up to you how you play your role. You might be a fighter who battles other clans or choose to gather materials and healing items while hanging back near your clan's den. This feline world is yours to prowl around.

DINOSAUR SIMULATOR

The first thing you will notice with Dinosaur Simulator is that players can fight amongst themselves. This means if you choose to play as a herbivore, you'll likely die to a large predator – unless you have a big spiky tail or horns to fight with. However, just because people fight each other, it doesn't mean you can't live a peaceful life and head out to the more wooded areas. Let's be honest, playing as the carnivores does mean much more excitement can be had. Imagine being a raptor who scurries around jumping into fights and claiming territory.

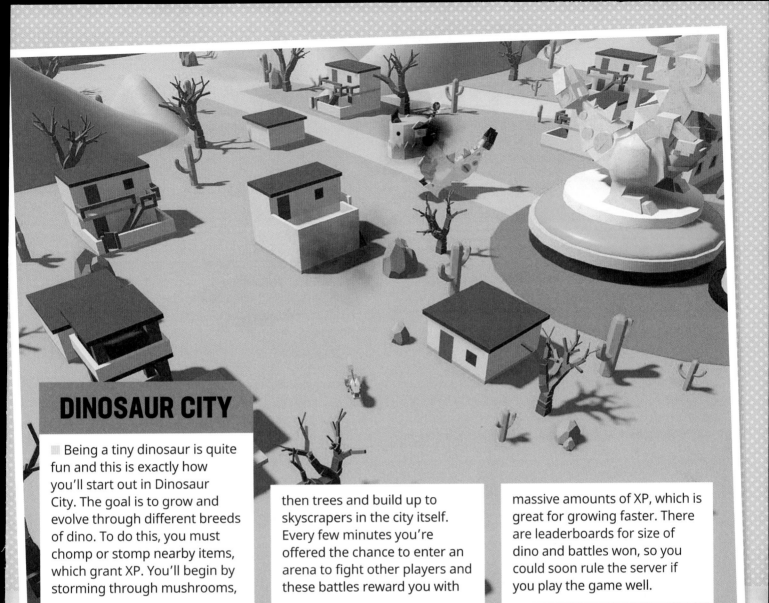

DINOSAUR CITY

▓ Being a tiny dinosaur is quite fun and this is exactly how you'll start out in Dinosaur City. The goal is to grow and evolve through different breeds of dino. To do this, you must chomp or stomp nearby items, which grant XP. You'll begin by storming through mushrooms, then trees and build up to skyscrapers in the city itself. Every few minutes you're offered the chance to enter an arena to fight other players and these battles reward you with massive amounts of XP, which is great for growing faster. There are leaderboards for size of dino and battles won, so you could soon rule the server if you play the game well.

ANIMAL SIMULATOR

▓ Animal Simulator differs slightly from Dinosaur Simulator – you can start as small animals and live out a life of survival. The goal is to earn XP and begin levelling up your animals. This can be done through fighting other players or within the training camp. As you level up, more animals become available and your chosen beast will become stronger and have more health. Once you hit level thirty, you'll be able to set up packs for others to join. Get some friends together and form a pride of lions, then head out and hunt the smaller prey that's roaming around. Can you rule the server as a powerful predator?

GOODBYE!

Well, what a trip through Roblox this has been! We've seen so many games, tried new experiences and hung out with friends. Roblox is a wonderful place, full of creativity and community. Maybe you come to try new games each day, or perhaps you feel inspired and want to try creating your own game. Whichever you choose, you're always home in Roblox.

So, what have we seen over the pages of this action-packed annual?

We've seen players versus other players, zombies chasing us through dark corridors, treasure chests found in piles of sand, and we've built boats from simple blocks. We casted spells, collected pets and did some relaxing farming. We got scared together, solved some mysteries and played a role in some big cities. We learned to fight, learned how to make money and learned what makes a great obby game into a huge hit.

Hopefully you've found some of your favourite games in these pages and you've also discovered a new favourite that you didn't know about before you opened this book. Remember, if there's a game you love, tell your friends and get them involved! The more people who play, the better many of these games will become.

Now you've finished reading, it's time to get back to playing. Stay safe online, be a respectful member of the community and remember, it's just a game.

SEE YOU NEXT YEAR!

STAYING SAFE ONLINE

YOUNGER FANS' GUIDE

Spending time online is great fun. These games might be your first experience of digital socialising, so here are a few simple rules to help you stay safe and keep the internet an awesome place to spend time:

• Never give out your real name – don't use it as your username.
• Never give out any of your personal details.
• Never tell anybody which school you go to or how old you are.
• Never tell anybody your password, except a parent or guardian.
• Before registering for any account, ask a parent or guardian for permission.
• Take regular breaks, as well as playing with parents nearby, or in shared family rooms.
• Always tell a parent or guardian if something is worrying you.

PARENTS' GUIDE

ONLINE CHAT
In most games, there is live on-screen text chat between users. Parents are advised to ensure that their children are only talking to friends and that they aren't being exposed to any adult matter.

SOUND
Sound is crucial in many video games. Players will often wear headphones, meaning parents won't be able to hear what children are listening to. Set up your console or computer to have sound coming from the TV or monitor as well as the headset so you can hear what your child is experiencing.

REPORTING PLAYERS
If you see or hear a player being abusive, Roblox allows you to report users or interactions. You'll be able to use the Report Abuse links found throughout the site on game pages, but there may also be buttons within chat windows or game menus where you can raise a case with community managers.

SCREEN TIME
Taking regular breaks is important. Set play sessions by using a timer. Some games can last a long time and if your child finishes playing in the middle of a round, they could leave their teammates a person short and lose any points they've earned. It is advisable to give an advanced warning for stopping play or clearly outlining a stopping point before any play session begins.

IN-GAME PURCHASES
Many games offer in-app purchases to enhance the game experience but they're not required to play the game. They also don't improve a player's performance. There are ways to set up safety measures on you child's account by setting up a PIN through Settings. Consult these before allowing your child to play any game in order to avoid any unpermitted spending on your account.